HOW TO GET THE BEST JOB OF YOUR DREAMS;
A quick and complete guide on winning your dream job

BY: LEO.G.WILLIAMS

Table of contents

CHAPTER 1

How do you know what job is right for you ?

Do you recall, when you were 18 years old, worried that you didn't know what you were going to do for your first job, let alone what you wanted to be when you grew up? That's very normal; the majority of us don't simply choose our ideal profession straight after high school or settle on a field in college and stick with it for the rest of our lives.

It's not quite possible to just Google "find dream job" or "what career is appropriate for me?" and receive a tailored response (yet). So how can you locate your ideal employment when you're unsure about your career path?

The TL;DR is that you should look at your strengths, consider who you are, communicate with others, educate yourself, take into account your requirements, and, at the end of the day, do what makes you happy. A recent Gallup survey found that 60% of millennials alone are considering changing careers (opens in a new tab).

Therefore, having the thought "I don't know what career I want" or even "I need a career change but don't know what to do" is by no means unusual.

It is one thing to understand that changing careers is a possibility (and possibly even unavoidable). But how can you determine what line of work or job to take when you're ready for a change? It's really simple to lose interest in a career or job you're not particularly thrilled with and pass up a dream opportunity without even recognizing it.

So how can you avoid finding yourself in a career rut? And how can you determine which long-term job route is best for you when there are so many options available? What steps can you take to address the question, "What career is right for me?"

HOW CAN YOU TELL WHICH JOB IS BEST FOR YOU?

1. USE YOUR STRENGTHS TO LEAD;

You can still know what you're good at even if you don't know what career you want to pursue. Making a list of your strengths is a terrific method to concentrate on your abilities. If you're not naturally good at that, get a friend's or a trusted coworker's opinion. You could also use a tool for

self-analysis like the Myers-Briggs
personality test.

An effective strategy to determine a
professional path that will match and
complement your skills is to actively
consider what you are good at and what
makes you tick from a personality
perspective.

Of course, if you work hard enough or put in
enough time, you can succeed at everything.
But if you let your strengths guide you to
what you should be doing rather than
forcing yourself into a career that doesn't
really suit, you may save a lot of time and
avoid aggravation.

For instance, you might have persuaded
yourself (or allowed others to persuade you)
that you're not good at arithmetic only to
discover that you enjoy applying logic to
difficulties.

In that situation, you may discover that you are passionate about a subject like web development that you may have previously dismissed. It's simple to allow preconceived notions to prevent you from pursuing a successful IT job, but if you take the time to examine your skills, you'll probably be pleasantly pleased by what they reveal about you.

2. Assess your history to prevent a dead end.

Answer the following questions on each job you've held to help you better understand your thoughts on previous positions so you can look for similar or different qualities in the future:

What aspects of the business did I appreciate and dislike the most?

What aspects of the business culture did I appreciate and dislike the most?

What aspects of my boss did I enjoy and dislike the most?

What aspects of the persons I worked with did I like and dislike the most?

What aspect of working there was the most difficult?

When was I most content or proud?

What was my greatest success?

What aspects of my responsibility did I enjoy the best and the least?

Examining your past might also aid you in remembering crucial occasions that you might have missed but that would have made it evident that you weren't satisfied with your performance. It's time to move on if looking back starts to reveal unfavorable trends regarding a particular profession or career.

There's a good chance that you're passing on opportunities elsewhere that would be a far better fit for your requirements and skills. Finding the kinds of conditions that will bring out your best work and happiest self requires a lot of analysis of your past experiences.

3. DISCUSS YOUR DREAM JOB WITH PEOPLE TO LEARN WHAT IT IS.

To learn about their career paths and gain professional guidance, start setting aside time during your job search to seek and schedule informational interviews with people in the sectors you're interested in. Inquire about their position, professional history, future goals, and the sector.

To make the most of these meetings or conversations, be sure to prepare questions in advance. In addition to saying "thank you" profusely when the meeting or call is over, do everything in your power to find a method to return the favor.

And don't restrict yourself to those you are acquainted with or have connections with. Attend conferences and workshops to network.

Join Facebook groups, other social media sites, or Twitter chats. Read job descriptions on LinkedIn or articles and interviews about people who hold positions you admire.

For instance, if you're interested in learning more about a typical day in the life of a WordPress developer, a quick Google search will probably turn up plenty of resources (including a few podcasts) and contacts you can use.

Make sure you get a sense of what the job
entails on a daily basis before you decide on
a career path or completely rule something
out.

4. ENROLL IN CLASSES FIRST, THEN DETERMINE YOUR NEW CAREER

time an occasion arises, try something new.
Attend workshops, read books, watch
YouTube tutorials, and take online lessons.
By taking these chances, you might discover
that you're truly like Python programming,
digital marketing, UX design, or something
else different!

The point is that there are so many
opportunities for learning new skills
nowadays. By utilizing them, you have a
great chance to discover a passion that will
provide you more career flexibility, help you
obtain employment, or that you can turn
into a new profession.

Aside from that, you'll at least have a new skill you can use to your existing position and perhaps even get paid more for, or a new interest you can convert into a side business.

5. ASSESS THE WORK ENVIRONMENT YOU REQUIRE

Are employees at the potential workplace either cooperative or in competition with one another? Do they get along outside of work? Do they collaborate or do they work alone? Do people have to work in the office or are they allowed to work remotely? How is the balance between work and life? What are the anticipated salaries?

When you are looking for that dream job to explore various career options or to completely change careers, these are all crucial questions for prospective workplaces and employers.

It's also a good idea (and simple) to conduct some preliminary research on your own, using Google searches and job boards to see what a typical job offer from job postings in your desired field looks like. This will help you learn more about industries in general and employers in particular.

Finding a company that values a collaborative approach is crucial if you are aware of the fact that you perform best in a team environment. Freelance or contract job that enables you to manage yourself and set your own conditions may be more beneficial if you're more productive working alone or you dislike the full-time grind.

Concerns about flexibility and schedule are equivalent. Look for a regular, 9–5 work in an office setting if you do best in a structured environment and appreciate reporting directly to a boss for direction.

However, considering remote employment will be essential to your career happiness if you like the freedom of working from home or while traveling as a digital nomad, and you're more at ease being your own boss or supervisor.

You can always attempt picking up side job to assist you figure things out if you are unsure of where you stand with these things. For instance, if you now work in a hierarchical workplace, try taking on some solo freelance projects and see if you feel differently.

The same is true if you typically work by yourself; try connecting with others instead, or work on a group project as a side project to see if you would enjoy teamwork more.

6. Follow your bliss, even if you're not sure

what that means for your career just yet.
Regarding your career, you should give the
following two questions careful thought:

What do you enjoy doing so much that you
would work for nothing to do it?

Consider this: Getting paid for something
you love so much you would do it without
being compensated is the very definition of
a dream job.

Try to visualize the "work you'd do for free"
before beginning to make connections
between it and paid opportunities available
in the same industry.

What (and not what would make you the
most money) would make you the happiest?
What result would you want to see if you
Googled "find dream job"?

You shouldn't always pick the most prominent career simply so you can wow people at cocktail parties, even if we all need to pay our expenses and, hopefully, still have money left over for a pleasant life.

Instead, select a career that will make you the happiest and allow you to develop and learn for greater long-term satisfaction.

Consider your true interests rather than what could seem to be the most profitable or high-powered job on paper.

Then, use those interests to direct you toward a suitable job path. Try to identify the things that fascinate you in such a way that you can always muster at least a spark of excitement for them.

The good news is that finding your dream career doesn't have to mean compromising your values or what you want from your professional life.

By using the aforementioned advice, you can have a clear understanding of what makes you tick professionally so that you can locate employment prospects and a career path that actually meets your demands and preferences.

Even while you might not think you know what you want, with some thought and perseverance, you'll quickly see that it is genuinely within your grasp.

CHAPTER 2

How to make the right approach for your dream job

Even if it seems impossible, most professionals have a dream job. Naturally, having a dream and actively working for it are two distinct activities. A dream is nothing more than a wish if you don't approach fulfilling it with intention and take small efforts to accomplishing goals that bring you closer to it.

What should your first move be to make it a reality?

1. make sure that postings emphasize specific requirements.

Find job listings that correspond to the title of your ideal position. Point out the qualifications or skill sets listed in the job posting that you lack.

Get to work right away honing those skill sets! Request to be put on assignments right away that will help you develop those skill sets. Find relevant courses or credentials so that you can complete all the requirements when the time comes to apply.

2.Track Your Successes

Keeping track of one's accomplishments on a monthly basis is one of the most crucial things someone can do today to progress toward achieving their ideal job.

Quantifiable accomplishments are hard to recall in the future, so be sure you're tracking and recognizing them as you go.

3. increase your visibility

Join a professional membership group in your ideal industry to increase your visibility to others who hold that position. Participate in conferences, serve on committees, and look for mentorship.

This will increase your visibility and build your network while also expanding your understanding of the field, giving you greater perspective and self-assurance as you pursue your ideal job.

4.Position Yourself To Pivot

It's simple to become bogged down in the planning phase when chasing a desire. However, positioning is more important than planning.

Ask yourself, "What are the crucial behaviors that need to happen consistently in order to pivot into my desire?" Imagine your dream as a pivot that you must prepare for. Be a Santa Clause: Make a list and double-check it. Behave properly and move toward the pivot.

5.Change How You View Expectations

Reframe your expectations of a "dream job," which will leave you disappointed when the ideal is ruined by unavoidable flaws. Instead, pay attention to the numerous fantastic professions that are available, including the one you want the most.

Set attainable objectives, such as updating your résumé and cover letter. You never know when a job posting will become available, so be prepared!

6.Watch The Gap

Finding your current position in relation to your ideal job is the next step once you are aware of what it is. Find people who are already doing the job you want, and ask them what qualifications they feel are necessary for success in that position.

Create a plan to close the gap between your existing skills and those required for your dream career after considering the difference.

7.Create A Strong Network Within The Sector

The first step in securing your dream job is building a strong network in the field you are hoping to work in. Make sure you are well-versed in the leading authorities in your industry and keep up with the trends that will enable you to see any possibilities that may arise. Stay informed and educated. When positions open up, employers will think of you first.

8.Plan out your ideal career

Find 10 job descriptions for the position you want. Draw attention to the qualifications that the recruiting manager for your ideal job is seeking.

List the most popular terms, abilities, and certifications that you might need to obtain. Start acquiring knowledge that will better position you for the move, such as new skills or certificates. Make finding your dream career your first priority.

9.Keep your sights set on the goal.

Despite our interest in and conviction about our ideal jobs, there is so much competition for our attention that we can easily lose track of it each day.

Having a photo or image of something that reminds you of your ideal career can be useful as a visual cue to help you focus on it.

CHAPTER 3

How to apply for a job

A job application is what?

A group of documents you submit to a business or organization where you'd like to work is known as a job application. The majority of the time, job applications also include a cover letter, a list of references, and any additional materials that will assist hiring managers learn more about you as a candidate, such a portfolio of your work.

The most typical way to apply for a specific position that has been posted with a job description is to submit a job application.

The job application process is sometimes the first step that comes to mind when considering how to apply for a job. You might receive an invitation to schedule an interview or to finish a take-home task after submitting.

Even though every firm may have a different hiring procedure, you'll nearly always need to explain who you are, where you've worked, and why the company is interesting to you in some way. This is typically accomplished by submitting a résumé, cover letter, and/or references at the beginning.

How to Look for a Job

More and more Americans are turning to the internet as their primary source for job search. In their most recent job search, 79 percent of Americans used online tools, according to a 2015 Pew Research Center study.

Numerous websites exist for job searching, including Indeed, CareerBuilder, USAJobs, and Monster, to mention a few. A wonderful location to both locate jobs and get discovered by recruiters is LinkedIn. Look at the jobs section of the website of the company you are interested in working for.

Most business websites feature a tab where they list available job openings at the moment. To find out if there are any positions that haven't been posted yet, you can also get in touch with people you know who work there.

How to Investigate Businesses

There are several methods for researching businesses. Getting the basics right, such as the company's mission, base of operations, and size, is a smart place to start. Their website has this introductory information.

People are a valuable source of information about a company: Request to schedule an informative interview with a coworker, even if you don't know them. See if you can arrange a meeting with an acquaintance (or an acquaintance of an acquaintance) who works there.

Ask them about the company's culture and, if appropriate, whether any roles are about to become available. It's also acceptable to get in touch with someone you find online and ask them a few questions about what it's like to work for their organization.

Reading news articles in which a company has been mentioned will also help you conduct thorough study on it. This can be crucial if the firm you're considering applying to is experiencing a crisis. You might not find news of the company's impending bankruptcy on its website, but you'll probably find it elsewhere on the internet.

How to Prepare Your Resume

Unless it's your first job application, you probably have a résumé floating around. Even though entire volumes have been published on creating the ideal CV, we'll only brush up on the fundamentals here.

First off, it's critical to style your resume in a digitally friendly manner as the job application process grows more and more computerized. This implies that you can omit the resume's printer-friendly version.

Try a modern resume template instead to grab a hiring manager's attention. Links to press coverage or samples of your prior work are also acceptable in your resume.

But it's also crucial to keep in mind that many firms use applicant tracking systems to sort through resumes before a person sets eyes on them, so do so before the hiring manager even views your resume.

It's one thing to list SEO (search engine optimization) as one of your core competencies; it's quite another to demonstrate how you used that knowledge to add value to an organization in the course of your employment history.

This is how to make sure your resume is compatible with [any ATS] system: incorporate the best keywords throughout your resume 2-3 times, with at least one of those references falling within your Work Experience or Education section.

Once you have a resume that is suitable for digital use, you may upload it to a website that facilitates job searching. With websites like Glassdoor, you may apply for a job by just clicking the "Easy Apply" button after uploading your résumé. It really is as simple as pushing a button to apply for a job!

The best way to write a cover letter
You have the opportunity to elaborate on the abilities, characteristics, and experiences you stated on your resume in the cover letter.

When applying for a particular job, you might change a few lines on your resume, but cover letters are typically far more targeted.

Fortunately, you've already done some research after reading our "How to Apply for a Job" tutorial, so it will be simple for you to write a cover letter that demonstrates your genuine interest in and familiarity with the organization.

Before writing the cover letter, have a look at the job description as well so you can match what you say about yourself with what the employer is looking for.

Additionally, keep in mind that not every job application requires a cover letter. As a result, if you're pressed for time, you can give priority to the applications on your list that don't, then move on to the ones that do. By creating your ideal cover letter using this template, you can also save time.

Documents to Keep on Hand

Now that your CV is in tip-top shape and your cover letter is polished, there is one more thing you should have ready before you begin submitting applications: references. References are individuals that you've worked with or for in the past and who can attest to your competence.

Set aside some time to chat with a few people who you are convinced will be excellent references for you before starting a frenzy of job applications. Although most applications only ask for three references, it's a good idea to contact at least five or six.

You can then provide references that are appropriate for the various roles you might be applying for. Those who provide reliable references include:
i your previous employer
ii A coworker you shared a workspace with
iii A mentor or professor
iv an adviser for students
v Your boss

These 5 email templates to utilize when asking for references are an excellent place to start if you're unclear of how to go. These folks should be asked for their email address, phone number, current title, and current place of employment, among other pertinent information.

Application Submission Procedure

While it is possible to apply for jobs in person or by mail, applying online is by far the most popular method.
Applying for jobs on the platform is made simple by uploading your resume online; the same is true for sites like Indeed, Monster, and CareerBuilder.

Other employers may request that you submit your application through their own website. It may be necessary for you to manually enter information from your resume on some company websites. We know it's uncomfortable, but there are occasions when you simply must do it.

Finally, many job postings include the recruiter's email address and request that you submit your CV and cover letter to apply. Our recommendation: Give that email some thinking! Don't merely state,

"Please find attached my cover letter and résumé." Give the recruiter a little additional information about yourself and your reasons for applying for the job as you express your gratitude for the opportunity.

Follow-Up Procedures for Job Applications After completing your application, it would be fantastic if you were given an interview invitation right away. You don't need to read this step, which is wonderful. But many of us have experienced the frustration of submitting a lengthy job application and then having to wait weeks or even months for a response.

If you have the recruiter's or hiring manager's email address, send a quick email to check on the application's status and to reiterate your interest in the position after waiting a week for a response. "Another brief, one- to two-paragraph message is in order, demonstrating real interest in the post and requesting the next steps if another week passes and you still have not heard from." I advise conducting research on contact names associated with the specific position or division for which you applied if you don't already have an email address for someone at the organization.

Send a brief note to that person telling them how you've applied to a position in this person's company, and are reaching out about a status inquiry. Keep it polite and enthusiastic, and hope for the best.

Let's take another situation. Say that you applied and were either rejected or didn't hear back from the company. A few months have passed, and you notice the same position posted again.

Should you apply? Yes — depending on the situation. Here are a few scenarios in which you might reapply:

You've remade yourself for the role with a comprehensive update of your résumé, cover letter and LinkedIn profile

The job had already been posted for a few weeks when you initially applied (thus your resume maybe got lost in a sea of hundreds of others) (so your resume potentially got lost in a sea of hundreds of others)
You've made more career advancements that you can contribute.

CHAPTER 4

How to Pass a Job Interview Successfully

One of the most crucial steps in the hiring process for a job or internship is an interview. Both the interviewer and the candidates might find common ground and ask questions throughout the interview.

The company evaluates your credentials, level of motivation, and whether you comprehend what you hope to gain from this position throughout the interview.

If you think of interviews as having benefits for the candidate, you may use them to assess whether a company aligns with your objectives and expectations.

Additionally, preparing for an interview is a fantastic method to hone your self-presentation skills, which are crucial in today's society.

You must adequately prepare for the interview in order to ace it and minimize any unexpected queries from the hiring manager. We can aid you there with our advice.

STEP 1: Do some background study about the business and the interviewers.

You can succeed in the interview by having a thorough understanding of the particulars of the organization you are applying for.

You will be able to determine how your experience compares to the data the firm has made public on its website and in social media, as well as what specific aspects of your experience make you a strong candidate for the position.

Step 2:Practice responding to typical interview questions

A popular interview question is, "Tell me about yourself and why you are interested in this position with our organization." Prepare your response. It's your personal elevator pitch, and the goal is to succinctly describe who you are and the value you will offer to the organization and the role.

Step 3:REVIEW THE JOB DESCRIPTION

Additionally, we advise you to become familiar with the job description beforehand and highlight the most important criteria for the applicant. Consider anything in your recent or former experience that satisfies these requirements.

Step 4: Have samples of your work available.

You will be questioned throughout the interview about particular jobs that you have completed in the past. Be ready to give instances of specific situations that relate to the job's requirements.

You might be asked, for instance, to describe a time when you worked in a team. Consider a specific instance and provide a succinct but useful description of it. Be ready for clarification questions about this case from the recruiter, so be familiar with it.

The recruiter analyzes your actions in the aforementioned circumstance and "translates" them to your conduct at work.

Step 5:Plan your route in

It is crucial to be at the interview on time, therefore we advise you to plan your route ahead of time and, if this is a new location for you, visit it once to familiarize yourself with it. By doing this, you can ensure that you won't be running behind schedule on the day of the interview.

Dress for interview success in step six. The outcome of your job interview can be greatly influenced by the first impression you provide to a potential employer. As a result, it's crucial to dress appropriately for the workplace.

However, the formal appearance will never be as stylish as the basic look (shirt, slacks, and shoes) (sweatshirt, jeans, sneakers).

STEP 7: Apply the STAR approach to your question-answering

Use the STAR method to tell stories with a clear Situation, Task, Action, and Result in case you are asked about instances in the past when you applied a particular skill.

STEP 8:The impact of body language

Crossed arms can be intimidating and appear defensive. Being focused and confident will instantly make an impression on your interviewer.

STEP 9: Create thoughtful interview questions.

An interview involves both parties. Employers want to know that you are really considering working there, so they anticipate you to have questions. You might wish to think about posing the following queries to your interviewers:

What will be my day-to-day duties in this position?

What metrics would be used to evaluate my performance if I were in this position?

What best describes the culture of the team?

What will the selecting process' next stage be?

When the interview is over and the recruiter has answered all of your questions, you can indicate that you have no further questions and thank him for the meeting if there are none left. It is best for candidates not to ask about pay up front.

If the recruiter did not inquire, it indicates that he already knows this information or that he plans to clarify it at the following phases of the selection process.

STEP 10: The impact of body language

Crossed arms can be intimidating and appear defensive. Being focused and confident will instantly make an impression on your interviewer.

STEP 11: Be upbeat and friendly.

Smile.
Even though an experience happened in the past, you shouldn't discuss it negatively. If the hiring manager does inquire about this, be as objective as you can when answering and focus on the positive takeaways.

Step 12: Try to manage stress

Don't try to concentrate on bad thoughts. You can picture someone you know sitting there in front of you rather than the recruiter while you describe your experience to him. You'll experience more comfort and self-assurance as a result.

CHAPTER 5

How to close a job deal

A strong résumé and cover letter may earn you an interview while you're looking for work, but your interpersonal abilities will frequently land you the position. Regardless of how well the interview went, you must have a compelling conclusion if you want to move on to the next round of interviews or receive a job offer.

It takes confidence and aggressiveness to close the deal during a job interview, as well as interest in the firm and consideration for the interviewer's time.

Leave a favorable impression on the interviewer

People frequently create ideas about others within the first few seconds of meeting them, therefore first impressions are obviously essential. The way you wrap up the interview matters just as much. Even if you thought the interview was a complete failure, don't let it show in your body language.

Firmly shake the interviewer's hand and maintain eye contact. Instead, smile, express gratitude for the interviewer's time, and then exit the room like you simply nailed the conversation.

Pose Serious Questions

Employers typically ask candidates if they have any other questions as they wrap their interviews. This is your chance to differentiate yourself from the competitors.

It's a "chance to look like a leader and show that you are interested in the interview," according to career strategist Cynthia Shapiro. Ask inquiries that demonstrate your interest in finding out more about the business and determining how you might help it expand.

Ask, "What are you searching for in an ideal candidate?" as an example. and "How does this position align with the long-term goals of the company?"

Offer recommendations

Don't only describe your abilities, credentials, or even professional successes; instead, inspire the employer to consider how you'll have a beneficial impact on the future of the business. Make a list of ideas on how you might carry out your job responsibilities based on your anticipated responsibilities as well as the demands and long-term goals of the organization.

Make Plans for Follow-Up

Ask the interviewer if you may follow up with them in a week to conclude the conversation. This demonstrates to recruiters that you have the confidence and drive to take charge of your professional life, which may transfer to drive and initiative on the job.

Because he anticipates your call, the interviewer is also more likely to keep you in mind while assessing applicants.